# Where I'm From

Written
by
Chante Thomas

Illustrated
by
Jennifer Price Davis

Copyright © Chante Thomas
All rights reserved.

ISBN: 1983690589
ISBN-13: 978-1983690587

## Dedication

To my mom, aka, Grandma Leatrice,

Thank you for all of the wonderful journeys as a child… the world became a much smaller place because of you.

I am Dawn.

The city of bridges is my home.

We have many kinds of bridges across the Cuyahoga River.
They swing, lift and soar!

The Cleveland Flats is home to lots of moving bridges.

Cleveland, Ohio is my home.

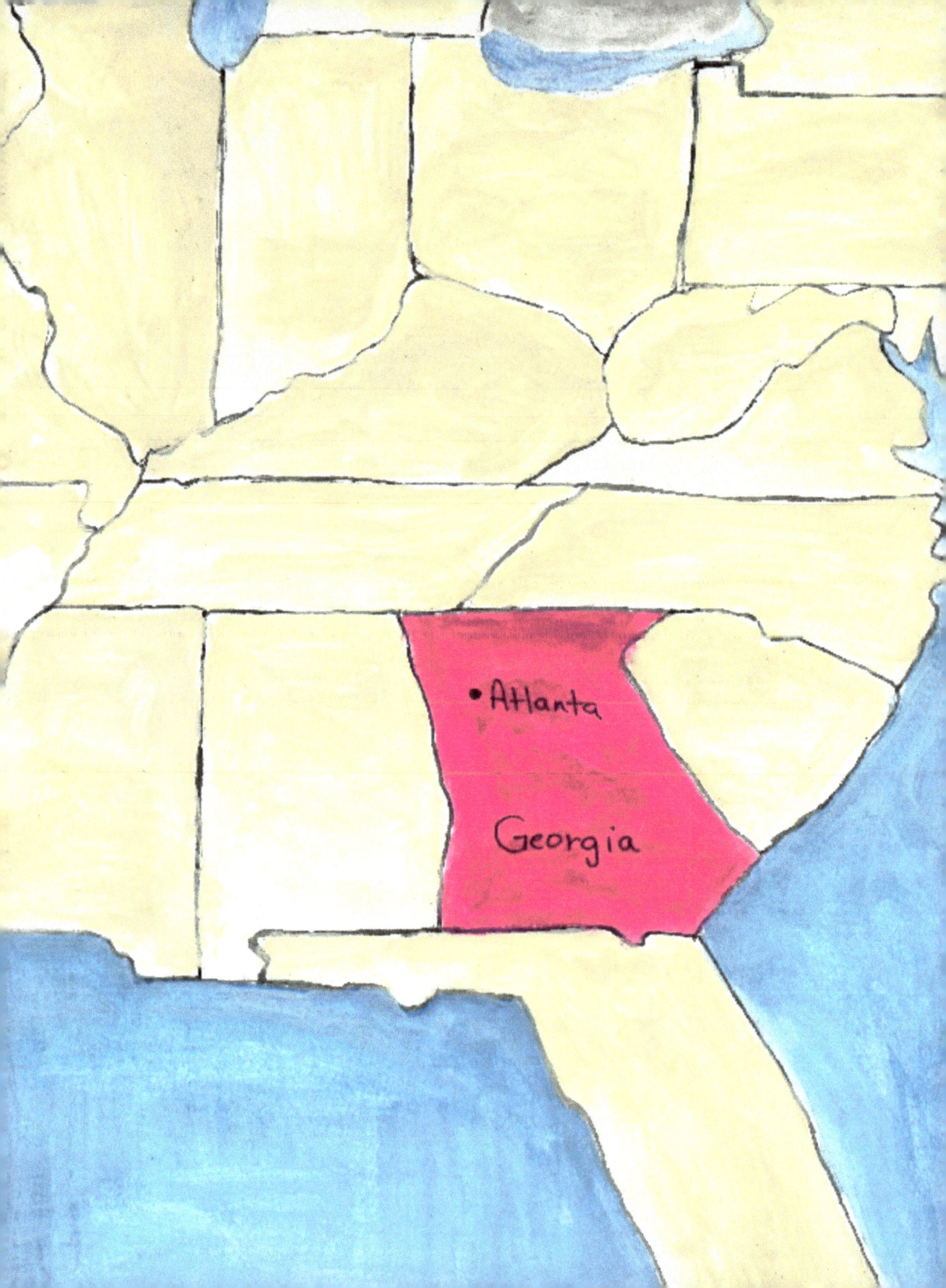

My parents are from Atlanta, Georgia.

Maybe that's why I say "water" funny.

But the best thing about my southern heritage is the way we do things. We are an African-American family.

I have the best of both worlds.

I am Casey.

I live in the Windy City.
Chicago is on Lake Michigan.

The winds that bounce off
the lake can knock you down
if you're small like me.

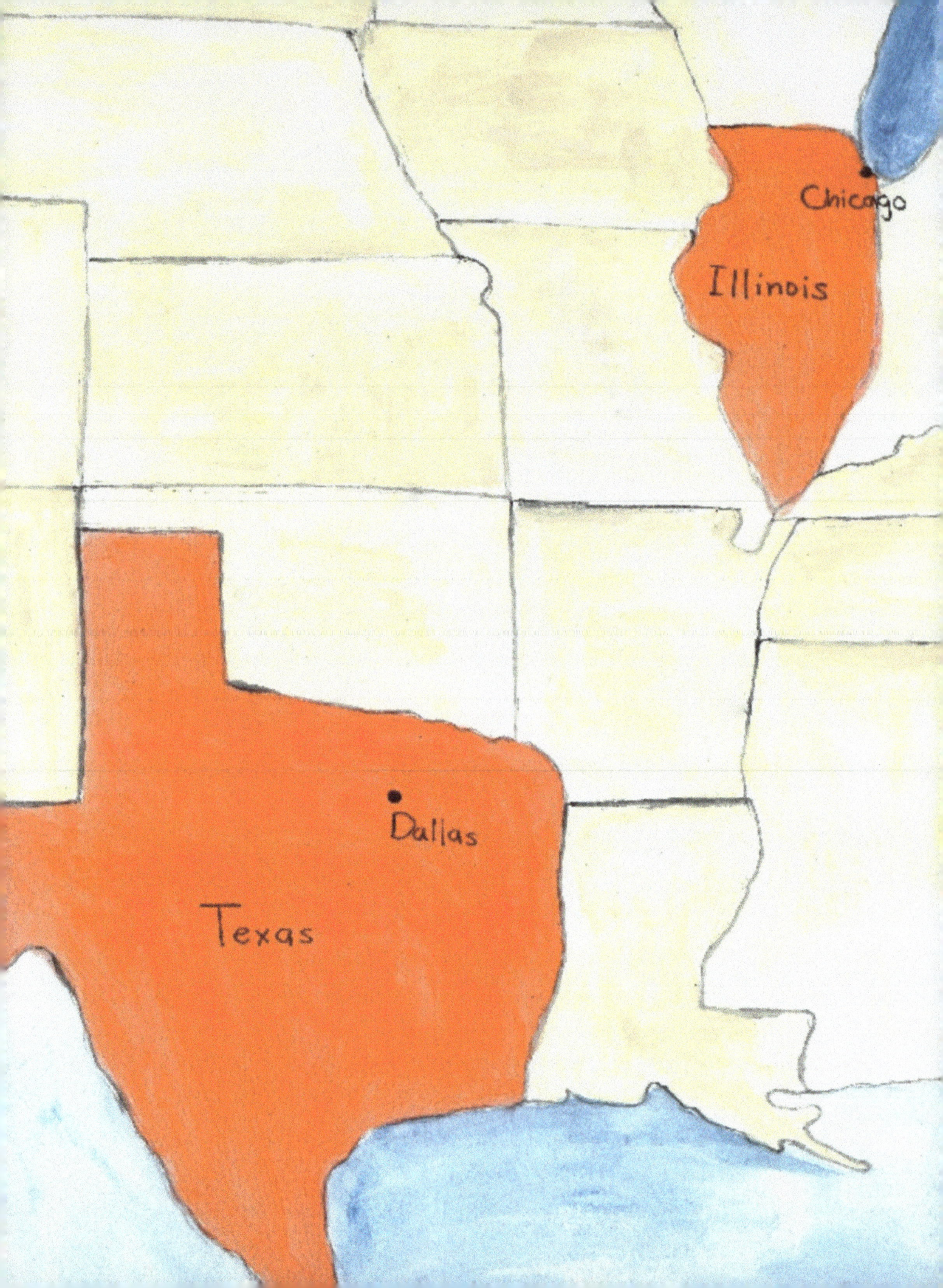

My dad is from Dallas, Texas. He is European-American.

His ancestors are from England. My mom is African-American.

My grandparents live in Chicago too.

We spend lots of time together.

I look like my dad, but I have my mom's personality.

My parents tell me I'm biracial and I too have the best of both worlds.

I am Reid.

My mom named me.

It's her maiden name.

Bonjour!

New York

New York

I was born in New York City.

Many call it The Big Apple. It's really an Island off the Hudson River.

To drive to New York City, you must drive on a bridge over the river, or drive into a tunnel which takes you through the river.

My parents are European-American.

My mom is from Baltimore, Maryland. She loves baseball!

My dad is from New York State. He lived on a farm when he was little. His ancestors are from Scotland.

Some people think New Yorkers are unfriendly, but I'll tell you a secret.

We're very friendly. It's just the words we say like, "Yo!" that fool people.

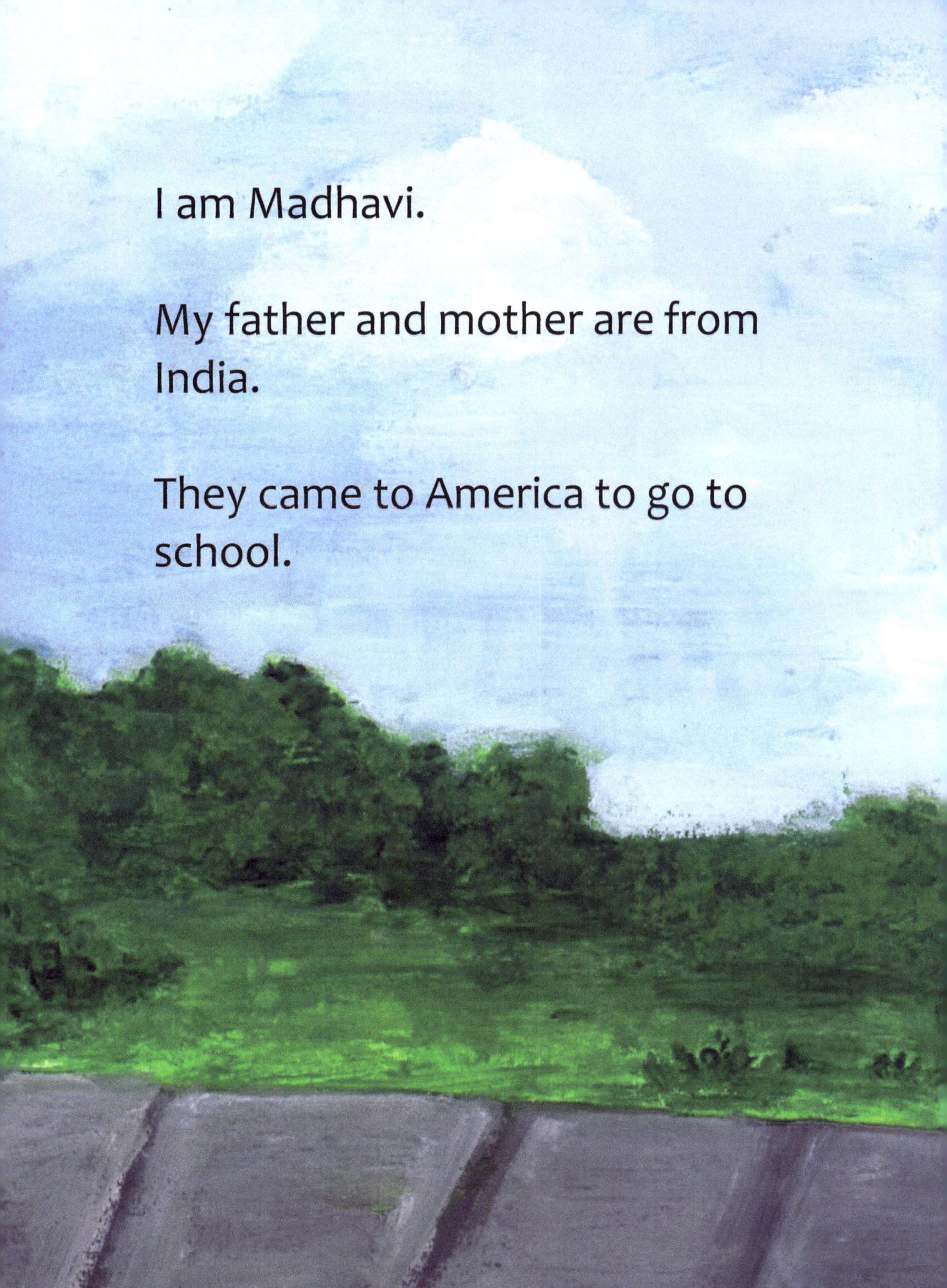

I am Madhavi.

My father and mother are from India.

They came to America to go to school.

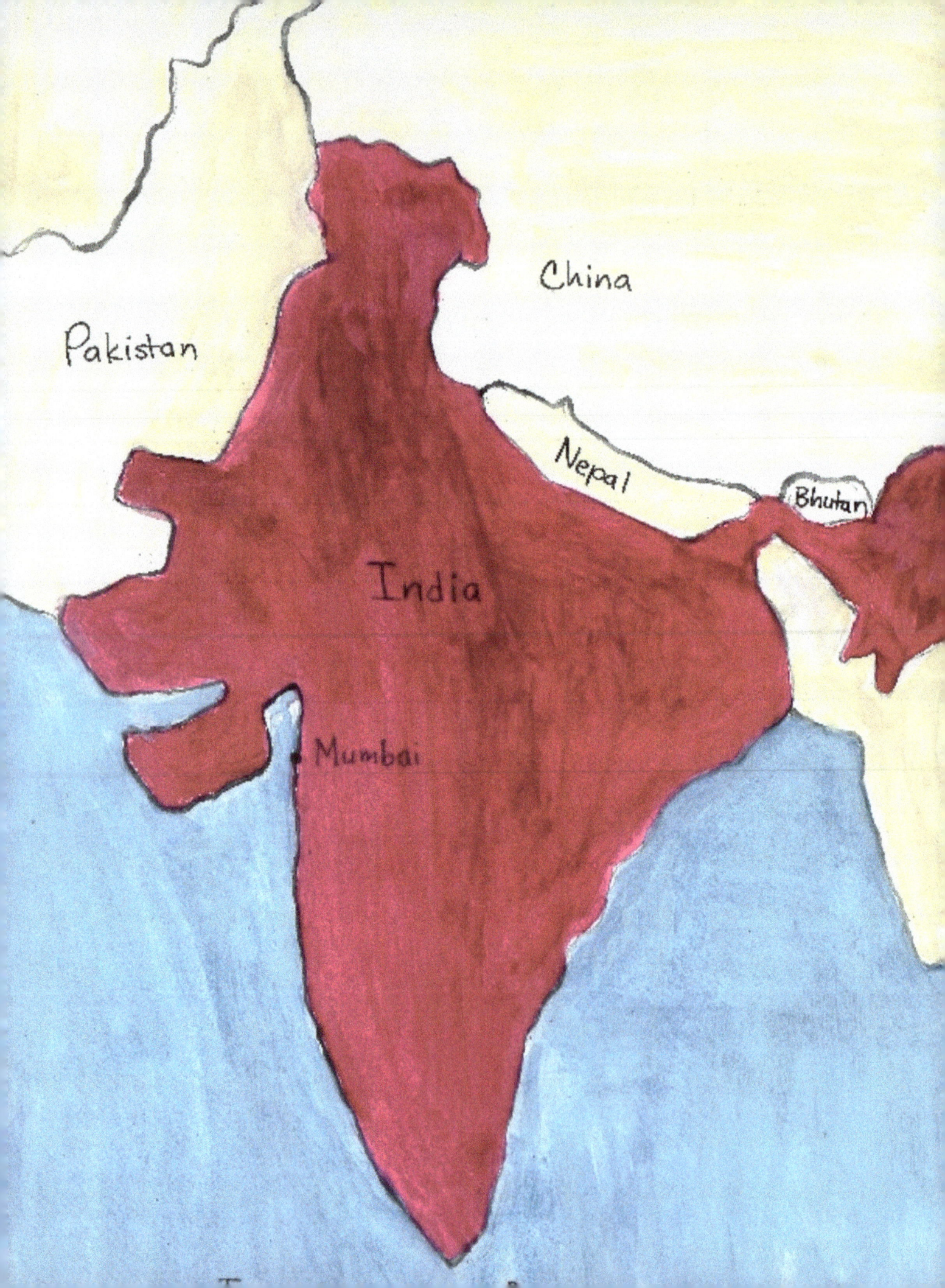

Their parents still live in Mumbai.

It can take 20 hours to get there by plane.

My parents had an arranged marriage.

This means that their parents agreed that the children would get married one day.

I'm really glad about that because my mother and father are awesome.

We speak in an Indian dialect at home.

Sometimes school is hard for me because I think in one language and speak in another.

I live in Cleveland, Ohio now.

Don't you think I have the best of both worlds?

I am Viviane.

My parents come from Abidjan, a city in the Ivory Coast in Africa.

They make many things there like coffee and cocoa.

I speak French and English. I wear my hair in braids because this is a tradition in my homeland.

Don't you love my hair?

My parents came to America to attend the university here.

They fell in love and decided to stay. We live in the nation's capital, Washington, D.C. It is a beautiful city that rests near the Potomac River.

Many people here are from someplace else. "Where are you from?" is a common question.

My answer is not that common.

I'm from Washington D.C. and Abidjan, Ivory Coast, Africa. I have the best of both worlds.

Just like the characters in this book, we are all from someplace special.

No matter if you are from the United States, or someplace amazing in the world, this makes us who we are.

We are all special and unique.

How can you use a map to tell your own story?

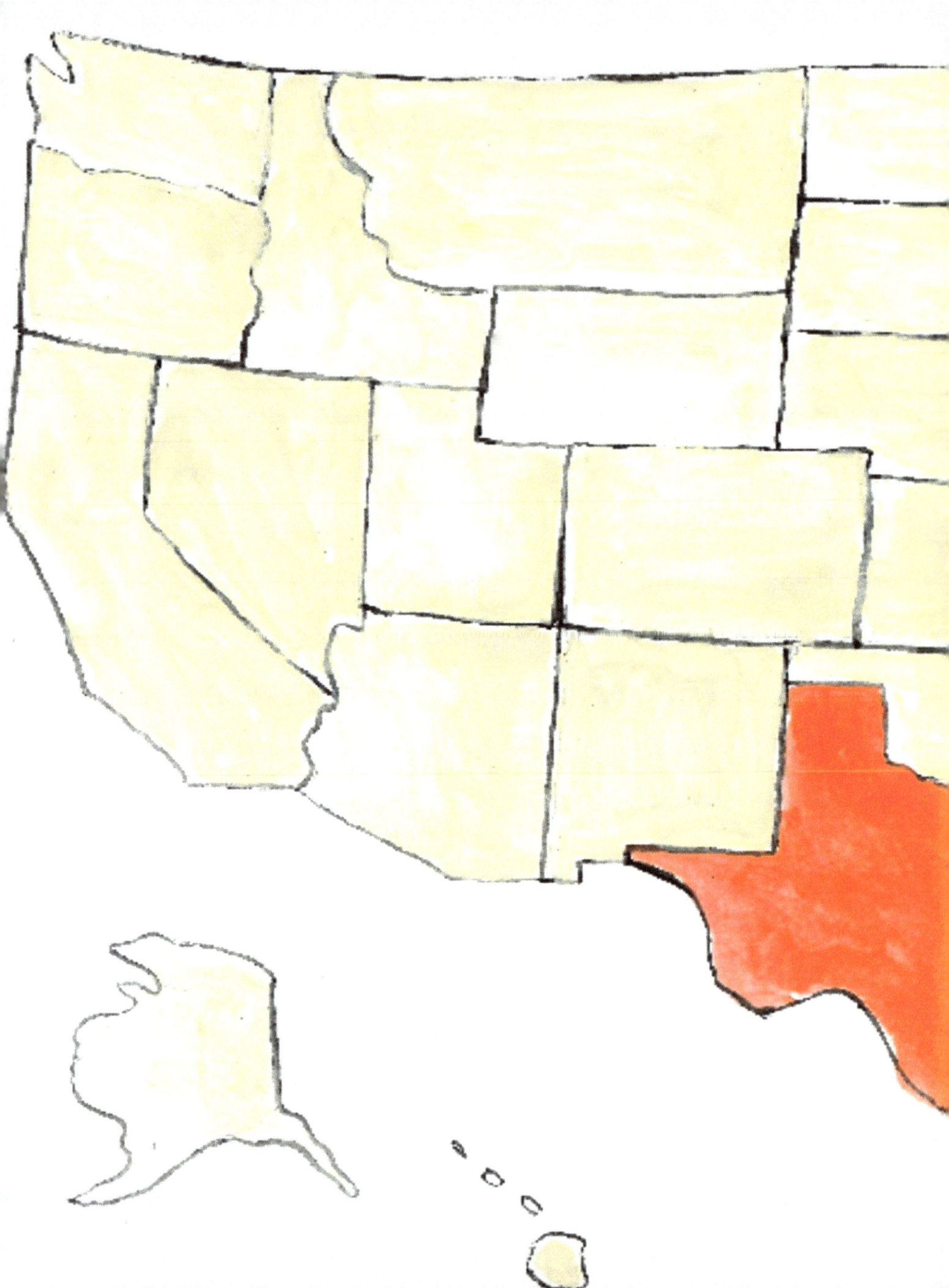

Tell us your amazing story!

I am...

## About the author

Chante Thomas is an elementary school teacher. This is her first published book; her love for geography inspired her to bring to life these wonderfully diverse characters. She has tried to instill in all of her students a sense of pride in knowing: whoever you are, wherever you come from and whatever your experiences are… you are amazing and have the best of both worlds.

www.ingramcontent.com/pod-product-compliance
Lightning Source LLC
Chambersburg PA
CBHW061114070526
44583CB00027B/3289